THE SEA TURNED THICK AS HONEY

HOLLY SINGLEHURST

Holly Singlehurst was born in 1993. After graduating with a BA in Music and English Literature from the University of Birmingham, she went on to complete a Master's in Creative Writing. She was commended in the National Poetry Competition in 2016 for her poem 'Hiroshima, 1961', shortlisted for the Bridport Prize in 2017, and recently won a Pushcart Prize for her poem 'On Agate Beach' (Pushcart Prize XLVI, 2022 edition). Holly lives and works in London. You can find Holly on Twitter: @HJSinglehurst.

'God had the book of life open at PLEASURE

and was holding the pages down with one hand
because of the wind from the door.
For I made their flesh as a sieve

wrote God at the top of the page'

Anne Carson, God's List Of Liquids

NOTES AND ACKNOWLEDGEMENTS

'The girl's monologue' contains italicised excerpts of a quote from the composer Henryk Mikołaj Górecki ('I wanted the girl's monologue as if hummed...on the one hand almost unreal, on the other towering over the orchestra.'), regarding his composition 'Symphony No. 3, Op. 36', also known as the 'Symphony of Sorrowful Songs' (1976). 'The Physical Impossibility of Death in the Mind of Someone Living' borrows its title from the 1991 Damien Hirst work of the same name. 'Purple Rain' borrows its title from Prince's 1984 song; 'All Shook Up' does likewise from Elvis Presley's song of 1957. The title 'Bring me my bow of burning gold, bring me my arrows of desire' is from William Blake's 'And did those feet in ancient time', now better known as the hymn 'Jerusalem'.

Many thanks to *And Other Poems*, and *Iamb*, where some of these poems first appeared. Thank you to The Poetry Society and the National Poetry Competition judges for commending 'Hiroshima (1961)' in the 2016 National Poetry Competition. Thank you also to the Pushcart Prize for selecting 'On Agate Beach' for publication in Pushcart Prize XLVI (2022 edition).

Thank you to the friends and family who have supported both me and my writing, especially those who read the earliest drafts of these poems. Thank you to all at *The Rialto*, particularly to Rishi Dastidar for his perceptive edits, enthusiasm, and unfaltering belief in my work. Thank you to Luke Kennard, for his encouragement right from the start. To those without whom these poems could not and would not exist, thank you. And thank you to Oli, my very best friend.

First published in 2021

The Rialto, c/o 74 Britannia Road, Norwich, NR1 4HS, United Kingdom

© Holly Singlehurst.

ISBN 978-1-909632-13-4

The Rialto is a Registered Charity, No. 297553

Typeset in Berling 9.5 on 12pt
Design by Starfish, Norwich
Printed in England
Cover image 'Flow' Nick Stone
The Publisher acknowledges financial assistance from Grants For Arts.

Supported using public funding by

LOTTERY FUNDED | ARTS COUNCIL ENGLAND

CONTENTS

EXOSKELETON

I live in my socks and shoes the way I live in my hands,
the gloves of my skin, my soft grey jumper and
baggy jeans. A snail moves slower knowing its home
is always there, on its back, to retract its jellied body into,
the way I curl myself into you, our bones buried deep inside.
In this way we are unlike the hermit crab who chooses his shells:
broken bottle, plastic cup, sea glass. See glass as a window,
as something smashable, the way an angry man could smash
a plate or any one of my finger bones. Last night I went walking
in the dark, the rain slick pavement, the smell of not-quite-night.
Two snails were curled together, their shells nervously bumping
like teeth in a first kiss. They were making something like love
before they crunched so easily under my foot.

LUNCH DATE

I went out for lunch with the rain.
She was quiet, handsome, she changed
the light in the room. Everyone could
feel her presence, even with their backs
turned towards her. I kept trying
to make jokes, but she didn't laugh,
just rained heavier onto the table.
When I smiled, she smiled, but she
had no mouth. She was only water,
filling and filling my cup.

STAGE FRIGHT

You're not here in this room
but I've carried you with me,
worry stone in my pocket
smoothed by your thumb,
headache in my dumb heart
throbbing its wet red aria
round and round and round.

The human heart starts beating
when it is the size of a grain of sand;
a snake can slide theirs up and down the body
to protect it, not from its own predators,
but from their prey as it is swallowed down.
This is possible as they have no diaphragm,
unlike mine which used to shudder
my chest every time I sang a note
so I or someone else had to hold it,
steady hands beneath my rib cage,
let the vibrato come from the throat.

The audition panel ask me to
sing it again, but really feel the beat,
suggest I use my fingers to tap
the rhythm back into my chest,
little blood metronome tick tick tick –

A WOMAN IS CRYING AT THE TIP

Throwing chandeliers into a skip
from the top of a flight of stairs.

She thinks of ballet, how bodies
land on the stage without breaking.
It is the audience that shatters.

WITCH BURNING
After Sylvia Plath

Her mouth makes the sound of a kettle whistle –
high, sharp, spinning into air like smoke. I watch.
Everyone around her watches. Her body peeling back
on itself to reveal a wet heart, all of her beautiful organs.

When a man makes miracles happen he is God,
and when a woman walks on water she is burnt,
boiled to black bone, aware of her poached flesh
melting into flames – hot at her heels, inevitable.

They say she placed warm milk by her sleeping children
in case they woke up, blocked the gap under their door,
placed her head in the oven – thought sweet apple pie,
rack of lamb, fresh bread. She turned the gas on.

HUNDRED FOOT DRAIN

I want to tell you a secret thought I've been having.
The thought embarrasses me, which is why I want only you
to have it. The thought goes something like *If I was a dog,
I'd put myself down*. To drown is to swim too far underwater.
The sun bounces off the river and makes a pattern on your face,
a mask of bright lace which lights up your eyes from the inside.
I want to kiss you in all the obvious and less obvious places:
your eyelashes, the wrinkled point of your elbow, your knees.
A tree dips its long wooden fingers into the water.
If you were a bird, what bird would you be?

MY PHYSIO TELLS ME A JOINT CRACKING
LOOKS LIKE FIREWORKS ON AN ULTRASOUND

She says I am built like a Duracell battery.
She is trying to be kind about my muscles,
which are coiled tight and impossible to relax.
She uses other euphemisms – a brand new spring,
an over-tuned string on a violin, a hive of bees.
She says it makes me who I am, which she means
to be a kindness, but in this context seems cruel.
She puts on blue plastic gloves and says
she is going to test my pelvic floor.
My whole body winces, is a slick slab
on a chopping board and she is the knife.
When she holds my ankles and twists them,
the sad choir of my body betrays me.
I am popcorn in a microwave.
Her fingers taste like blue plastic gloves,
I bite hard until I feel her thumbs twitch.
In exchange for this, she offers me other analogies:
my bones are ill-fitting shoes, stiff zips, broken screws.
I am late, and a little drunk, to the party of my body,
anxious in the corner, rubbing my thumb against the lip
of my glass, and everyone else is dancing.
They are beautiful and freshly oiled as new bicycles;
they are drinking champagne, a mesh of bright bubbles and gold.
Their warmth against the cold steams up the windows
so from outside, the flashing lights behind their bodies
look like fireworks.

INSTRUCTIONS
After Gertrude Stein

Listen to me carefully, now.
Go to the mirror and take off your clothes.

     Take them all off.

Hold yourself in your arms and feel soft.
Place your fingers in your mouth and taste skin.

     Breathe out.
     Breathe in.

Close your eyes and repeat after me:
     A rose is a rose is a rose is a rose.

THE YELLOW CURTAIN (1915)
After Henri Matisse

Morning casts your naked shadow
against the back wall.
I can see every part of you,
still wet from the shower.

When I pull the yellow curtain
to hide my body,
you get down on your knees,
lick between my toes.

But when we fuck, I see everything,
                          you say.

I do not let go of the towel.

I WANT

your hair a damp blanket
draped over me

you to suck on my nipples
mouth latching like a lamb

your fingers slipping in
the way an orange peels

pain a promise of something
a tree bending in the wind

bent so far the branches
cling to the roots

hidden joints breaking apart
as salt dissolving into water

my desire second hand
second hand as in belonging to you

my second hand touching you there
until you become my second hand

I once saw a bird so small
and beautiful I thought it was a moth

feathered bullet against my window
it was so hungry for the light

I once pissed on my hand
just to prove I was warm

ODE AS YOU RUN ME A BATH

The pain bleeds from my jaw joint, curls itself
behind my eyes, blooms at my temples. I can't
crawl out of my skin, and the pills don't work.
When my body is aching, you make me soup.

You run me a bath with hot water, lavender soap;
the soft bubbles make a collar around my neck.
When I dip below the surface, I can hear my heart
beating in my ears. I am a bowl filled with blood.

The whole room sweats, the windows are steamed shut.
You take off your towel and step in. I ask if you know
how many litres of liquid there are in the human body.
You say nothing. You hold my face in your wet hands.

THE GIRL'S MONOLOGUE
After Henryk Mikołaj Górecki, Symphony of Sorrowful Songs

I

Of the second movement, the composer said:
I wanted the girl's monologue as if hummed.

A high human note can shatter glass but it must be the exact same note
as the resonant frequency of the glass.

Everything has a resonant frequency, the natural frequency at which something vibrates.

Researchers have found that the human body, as a whole, has a resonant frequency,
and that bones have their own individual frequencies.

Organs have yet to be tested, but we do give off radiation,
mostly infrared, which has a frequency lower than visible light.

II

When asked about the second movement, the composer said:
I wanted the girl's monologue as if hummed.

Monologue, from the Greek word 'monos', meaning 'alone',
and the Greek word 'logos', meaning 'speech'.

Monologue: for a single character to express their thoughts and ideas aloud.

The girl's monologue was to be hummed.   Lips closed.
He said he *wanted the girl'*

III

The composer said he *wanted the girl's monologue as if hummed,*
   on the one hand almost unreal, a frequency lower than visible light,
         to be in visible light.

For a human voice to shatter glass, the glass must have microscopic defects.
    Shatter: to break or destroy, to upset (someone) greatly.
    Origin: Middle English, in the sense to scatter/disperse.

The girl scattered her invisible light, divided her light into wavelengths.

She was to be *on the one hand almost unreal, on the other*
          towering over the orchestra.

THE TOPOGRAPHY OF TEARS
After Rose-Lynn Fisher

Last night, when you cut yourself,
you used a tissue for the blood,
a slim test tube for the tears.

This morning, you touch your body
until your fingers are soaking – softly,
slowly. Spread yourself onto a slide.

Underneath the microscope you study
your hidden shapes. The metal is cold
and hard. It digs into your socket.

On a white label you write
        pleasure.
    on another,
        pain.

You do not know where to place them.

BLUE WATER

I saw you by the water,
by the blue water.
You were washing
your bones.

You dipped them
beneath the surface,
twisted them, placed
them into my hands.

They were light as birds' bones.
They made my palms wet.

But these are your bones
                    I said.
You said,
I do not need them,
where I am going.

ALL SHOOK UP

I still like to use your death as an excuse for my most banal failings.
When I struggle to focus on emails, or to hoover the sitting room,
I think about how you killed yourself and that allows me at least an hour off.
In this hour, I make a cup of tea, put the radio on, spoon 100% peanut butter
straight from the jar and into my mouth. I am a woman in an advert for peanut butter.

I love writing about how we kissed in the rain, for hours, on a park bench in Brixton,
how we kissed like we were watching ourselves kiss in a film. The taste of your tongue,
heavy thumbs up my spine. I like to say you cried wolf, just love to forgive myself.
Your handful of pills, last bitter dry swallow, then silent and stiff as a bar of soap,
morning light through the slatted blinds splitting your tattoos with their golden knife.

You liked to feed me pasta with your fork, liked to lie to me and then laugh.

       You would sit on your balcony, smoking,
and look back at me through the glass doors like I was a fish in a bowl,
                      my tears the wet air of the room

until I was seven again, in the butterfly park's steaming hot tent,
wings big as dinner plates heavy on my arm and   I couldn't move.

                              I couldn't move

as you traced my outline with paint until your kitchen table was a mess of colour
      smudged   off the paper and onto the walls
                        your body
rubbed into the white carpet   the windows

                              smashed your clock

    timeless!   numbers everywhere   shards of   glass
                  you wouldn't stop   dancing
                      you wouldn't stop

sniffing the powder till your nose bled. *Turn the music up, up, up!!*
                You couldn't   *stop!*
                You couldn't stop.
You sang into your beer bottle, shook your hips, flicked your hair like you were Elvis.
          You were *all shook up*!   *Uh huh huh.*

It was so fucking funny.   *I'm in love.*

        You cleaved your arms open with the kitchen knife.

ON AGATE BEACH

A blue whale has fallen belly up
on the sand, and crowds of people
stand round with wet hair, hushed
voices, in their jewel bright shorts,

and the first woman I loved split
herself open from wrist to elbow and bled
out in the bath, up over its lip, slipped
under the heavy wooden door,

and the floor beneath my feet is tiny stones,
and bones, and broken glass worn by water;
and a whale's heart is as big as a car
and far more magical.

THE PHYSICAL IMPOSSIBILITY OF DEATH
IN THE MIND OF SOMEONE LIVING

The first time she saw the Greenland Shark she thought she was ugly,
I'm sorry she just looks rotten, she said, *clumps of flesh peeling off her.*
I like to think of her as mossy, like an ancient stone, replied the Marine Biologist,
who was also a wonderful saleswoman, *a great companion.* That sounded better;
besides, it had been a difficult year. Her soul felt soft as putty, brand new as an egg.
She liked how the Greenland Shark was older than anyone she'd ever met,
by hundreds of years – it was comforting, like someone's dad or a Professor,
but a female shark. *I'll take her*, she said, *alive.* She signed the forms,
paid the pre-arranged amount plus tax which was a lot but not too much,
all things considered. She watched the large net haul her out of the water.
When she got the Greenland Shark home, she wheeled her custom built tank
into the corner of her bedroom – like a large chest freezer in an American kitchen,
a sort of homage to Damien Hirst. *You'll like it here*, she told the Greenland Shark,
not looking up from the leaflet, working out how much and what she should feed her.
Surprisingly slow metabolism, she thought aloud. The Greenland Shark said nothing.
She put the radio on, BBC 3. It was playing Mozart's Requiem, the Lacrymosa.
From your younger years! she shouted over the music before turning it down.
She was embarrassed about the state of her bedroom. *Sorry about*, she gestured, *this.*
The Greenland Shark's eyes, frosted like a bathroom window, panned the room
to take in her surroundings. It was the first time she had ever seen above sea level,
having been tranquilised for the journey. The leaflet stated: 'Scientists estimate
the Greenland Shark is at least 250 years old, but potentially up to 500 years old.
They like to stay in the deepest, darkest parts of the ocean where it is very cold'.
She went to the ice machine to fill another bucket and tipped the ice into the tank.
You're going to keep me busy, she said, slapping the glass roof like a new car bonnet.
In the evening, she used the tank's light like a lamp, so everything glowed turquoise.
Sometimes she showed the Greenland Shark what it was like to have a human body,
to have arms and fingers and want. *I can never get there*, she said, frustrated,
can't relax into it. The Greenland Shark, with her blood-rich gills, was calm.
When she imagined the ocean's vast blue silence it made her cry. *These are tears*,
she told the Greenland Shark, hovering over the feeding hatch so they dripped
like rain into the salt water. When she was this close she had to block her nose –
the Greenland Shark, who she now saw as beautiful, smelt like a public toilet.
'Their bodies have high concentrations of urea; a necessity, to ensure they maintain
the same salt concentration as the ocean', explained the leaflet. She closed the hatch.
She liked to read late into the night, her back pressed up against the cold glass –
the classics, current affairs, personality quizzes. Her favourite was '36 questions
that may lead to love' – *Do you have a secret hunch about how you will die?*
she asked the Greenland Shark, *What could constitute a 'perfect' day for you?*
Most nights they took the quiz, leaving out the question which referenced telephones.
For what in your life do you feel most grateful? she asked, felt her pupils dilate.

LYSIS AND LAVAGE

I

After the operation
my body yawned open,
left to melt in the butter dish.

The salt water flushed out in its tide: cartilage,
scar tissue, fragments of loss. If you believe me –
memory, and light. My ear canal corked with jellied blood.

A body holds pain like copper coins,
saves it up and spends it, never all at once.
I unclenched my fist, opened my damp palm.

II

When the stiff bolt loosened, spun its way up and off the nail,
fell to the ground. When the nail itself fell out and left
a small hole, a perfect O, it let the light in.

Yellow sun splashed like milk on the dark soil.
I watered the seeds daily, as instructed,
until something shifted, a hard shell split,

cleaved open. A tiny clam, sprouting.
It pushed its soft green wick
up towards the light.

LIDO SONG

Come to me when your aching day
Has tied your heavy spine in knots
Your shoulders hunched your scraping knees

Strip off your suit your stiffened jeans
Your leather belt unlace your shoes
Stretch out and sigh and dive right in

Come to me my fizzing kids who clutch ice creams
Hot cups of tea in wilting paper cups
Picnic rugs and swimming floats and towelling robes

Painted angles of bright white lines
Clear blue shine my shock of cold my chlorine sting
Lengths you lose your body in to become all mind all mine

Then hold your breath pushing off to glide a length
And I will hold you till you rise
Return to air and sun and warmth and gravity and light

PURPLE RAIN

His silhouette lights up on a floating sheet:
                          think Gabriel, ascending; think Raphael,
                          stirring the waters of the healing pool.

Purple jackets and kohl, crystal buttons and high heeled boots.
Church of the stadium; church of the body, of bodies touching.

A chorus of screams bursts into light, lighter fluid,
                          skin slick with rainwater and sweat.

He is down on his knees. Read: confessional.
I am down on my knees, kissing your feet. Read: holy, repentance.

      Smoke of breath mixing   incense/d   O mist of our bodies.

You bring the blue and I the red, baby, believe me,
                 please believe me, *I know,*

I know, I know times are changing.

    You are a dark cloud, raining.   Amen, Amen.

Remember your childhood, the waves of the storm?

Your mum held your hair as you were sick over the side of the boat;
as I hold it now, you pressed into the cold porcelain of the toilet bowl.

              Honey, I know, I know, I know,

        you were held in the hand of God, his wooden palm,

rain as little wet shards,
    falling.

You are dew on my eyelash.   I only want to see you laughing.

LIGHT BUCKETS

If you want to catch rain, you use a bucket;
a bigger bucket, you catch more rain.
The same can be said for telescopes, which catch light:
the larger the lens, the more light it catches,
so astronomers call them 'light buckets'.

There's a hole in my bucket, dear Liza, dear Liza,
and the hole is a bright bulb trailing ribbons of gold on the carpet.
You, out in a thunderstorm, catching sparks in your cupped palms,
small suns burning rivers down your arms.

And laughter is simpler, shining from our eyes as pure light.
And a rainstorm at night sets the dry ground on fire.

THE HUMAN MICROBIOME

If every part of your body that isn't bacteria was removed,
there would be a perfect outline of you left.
A swarm of microbes, single celled and heartless,
all appetite, and enzymes, and irreverent multiplication.
We call this: the human microbiome. Within every swarm,
a Queen – her jewel armour, her sting, her dusty pollen
bright as sherbet and as sweet, her five glimmering eyes.
Surprising, then, that our organs continue their thankless work,
despite it all – pump alkaline blood, dissolve, contract and relax
each quivering notch of the throat. Offshore a boat hits rock,
her punctured side spilling dark tonnes of oil which spread
as smoke, float and choke and sink. Swimmers running out
of the grey stained surf are grateful they are built to breathe on land,
grateful for their particular, human biology. As I am now with you,
slick on my fingers like the sea turned thick as honey, wetter than water.

BRING ME MY BOW OF BURNING GOLD, BRING ME MY ARROWS OF DESIRE

I had a friend who gave blowjobs after school,
sheltered in the doorway of the Chapel.
Older men, pressed against the heavy latch,
growing hard in his mouth like a prayer or a fist,
like that hymn everyone knows, the organ
shifting its heavy keys into the chorus.
When he tells me this I am no longer a child,
but Madonna – Mother of Christ, Queen of Pop.
He is God, as a baby, in my lap.
Like a Virgin, I ask – what does it feel like?
He tells me how men like it when he cups their balls,
kneads them like bread; explains the thing he does
with his tongue to the tip, how he can feel
their shivers at the base of his own spine.
At the service no one can see our flames, how we
melt together. My mother, in the garden,
pours salt around her roses and has her suspicions.
I tell her a fact: that when a choir sings together,
their heartbeats synchronise. I tell my friend another:
how our teacher holds me in the dark, near the altar,
after everyone else has left the rehearsal.
The secret is sweet and fizzy; our laughter then,
unexpected, contagious, so close to God.

HIROSHIMA (1961)
After Yves Klein

In the street, I am warm past my summer skin,
the pavement is burning the soles of my feet.
My shadow copies me as I open my arms. When
I jump, it jumps, but it doesn't leave the ground.
The light through my closed eyes tells me
a secret, that I am the most beautiful red.
And another, that it has travelled millions of
miles, unobstructed, to touch only my body.

LOVE SONG FROM A SEASIDE SOUVENIR SHOP

Instead of telling you how much I miss you,
I send a small, funny magnet with a crab and a bucket,
a bouncy ball, sun warm stones from an empty beach,
sand sticky fingers from a soft, ripe peach and the glass clear water to clean them.

I send you a fat, heavy parcel of fish and chips, steaming in damp paper,
buttery flakes in crispy batter and just the right amount of salt and sauce.
I hand wrap the bath warm evening, write something short on a postcard
with pastel houses, and cut grey cliffs, and a first-class stamp.

For a moment, I'm torn between a wood carved seagull with your name on it
and the whole ocean, so I get you both. The blinding glint of sun on its surface,
the tight squinting smile of your eyes when you look right at it.

It's not on display, but I ask, and they have it – that secret sound the stones make underwater;
a solid bubble of your breath, so you can watch it rise up to the blue sky and break;
the best jellyfish, so small and domed and perfect that when you open it you'll say,
It's so pretty, it belongs in a bakery, and I'll laugh and say, *I know just what you mean.*